Poetry in the Park

Volume One

Edited By Maria Kamy Abdool
and Ron Howard

PublishAmerica
Baltimore

First printing

At the specific preference of the author, PublishAmerica allowed this work to remain exactly as the author intended, verbatim, without editorial input.

Photo on cover taken in Central Park, New York by Maria Abdool

ISBN: 1-4241-5232-1
PUBLISHED BY PUBLISHAMERICA, LLLP
www.publishamerica.com
Baltimore

Printed in the United States of America

The Authors of this book have agreed to donate all royalties from the sale of this book to the Children's Miracle Network

Children's Miracle Network is the alliance of premier children's hospitals. Every year, Children's Miracle Network hospitals treat 17 million children for every disease and injury imaginable. Children's Miracle Network hospitals impact the lives of more children than any other children's organization in the world. Children's hospitals provide state-of-the-art care, life-saving research and preventative education for children 24 hours a day, 365 days a year. There is a Children's Miracle Network hospital dedicated to serving children in every community across the United States and Canada. These hospitals are committed to providing the best care for children when they need it.

A Message to the Readers

by Maria Kamy Abdool

Welcome to our vivid journey.

Please have a seat besides me, join me, breathe with me; I am inviting you to sift through the pages of this penned treatise and capture with me each alluring thought, each magical reason, each embrace that were placed within each poem.

Let's formulate a song together, let's read between the lines and find a fairytale in each poem written by these wonderful authors. Join us as we color the world with our passion, with our talent, with our verses, with our words please join us as we move mountains within our imagination.

I can assure you that the sail ahead is a gentle one, no need to let your fears accompany you, feel free to let them vanish with the midst of the evening and come dream a dream with us. Let your days ahead gleam and glister as you're taken to paradise with our verses; Let our silken thoughts, images, verses be enough to carry you through a lonely day.

May our words be enough to shield you from the rain and encircle you with happiness in the middle of the night when the moon's beam is afraid to come out and greet you.

Mark a spot on the ground, right here besides me and let's commence our journey today. Let's sail with the rhythm of a song, while looking deeper and deeper within a sunset over the crimson sea. Come with me, let me take you to a place where you've never been, allow me to grant you the only wish you've longed for throughout the years.

Lie besides me, allow me to read to you, a magical poem that was written by a creative soul, let me allow you to get drenched with each vivid word while you're settled amongst lilies in a pond. Come with me, open your mind, your soul, your heart, your eyes, let me read to you a silhouette of words, soft and gentle, let me carry you across the evening sky. Hold my hand, let me take you between the stars; let's engrave your name on the edge of the moon.

I do hope the pages ahead are soft and enchanting and as magical as the first day of spring. I do hope you find strength, hope, love, and faith within our words in this poetry book.

Allow me to whisper in your air and carry you with me to the place I go to each night. Let your guards down and frolic with the waves with me; I do hope you are able to create a storm with our words and be able to shine with the morning sun. Come with me, silently, let us consume you, drift you, move you, settle you in the wilderness of time.

Today, tomorrow, and for the rest of eternity, let us share our laughter, bring forth your tears, shed your inhibitions, and dance with us as our verses come alive in your eyes. Lose yourself for but a moment and listen to the whisper of the pages as passion encircles you, feel the music come alive on your skin as her dreams are echoed through your heart and his desires leave an imprint on your soul. Permit yourself to indulge in your own secret smile as you compose a verse of your very own, let us inspire you. Our voyage is far from over, disentangle yourself from the world and let us ensue on an adventure as we lead you down the footpath of our reveries. Allow yourself to be consumed with fluttery anticipation with each turn of a page.

Dedications

A Thank You Note:

A special thank you to Ron Howard, you are truly exceptional, working with you has been great and I can only hope to do it again in the near future.

To Starlit, for always giving her love and support, her presence moves mountains for me.

A warm thank you to all of the authors Lainee, Rose, Mary, Jewell, David and Tom for coming together and allowing Ron and myself to put this book together.

And last but not least, I'd like to give my love to my one and only, Vp, you're my inspiration.

And finally, to all of my fans, especially at the SJU Early Stage Book Club.

Always,

Maria

Dedications

I would like to thank Maria Abdool for sharing her talent, ideas and time with me. She is an incredibly gifted poet whose talent is only overshadowed by her wonderful personality. Thank you for all you have done to make this book a reality.

To the very special poets who have contributed their work, their hearts and their souls to the creation of this book, you have my eternal gratitude and appreciation. Each of you holds a special place in my heart and it would take this entire book for me to express what you mean to me.

To my wife and children, I thank you for being my rock. You are the foundation that helps me weather the storms of life and I am nothing without your love.

To all who read this book for helping make the dreams of these new authors a reality.

Always,

Ron

Table of Contents

Maria Abdool

I am a published author, my first book is called 'Whispers in the wind' and the second one is called 'Bliss' which was published a few months ago. It's doing very well and I am very proud of my accomplishments. My upcoming project, 'Penned Sentiments' will be out in a month or so, and I am very excited to share my work with the world. I feel like I am giving a piece of myself in my poems and whoever reads my work, they can truly understand what I mean by saying that. I always write from personal experiences and use my knowledge to shower and embrace my readers.

I graduated from St. John's University in May of 2000 with a PharmD. and is now a Pharmacist at Medisys Health Networks. In May of 2005, I graduated from St. John's University with a Master's Degree in English Literature. I would like to further my studies in the coming future, but as of right now, I would just like to sit back and take everything as they come.

I started writing at the age of seven and always wanted to be published, that was my main focus, I wrote for a few public newspapers in my hometown, and also for my High School news-paper and I was always complimented on my writing talent.

There are many things that I love about life, but on a more personal note, I am in love with the most wonderful man, he makes me whole and you will find that I write about him in almost all of my poems. He's mainly my inspiration and because of him, I find it really easy to get lost in my verses when I choose to put them down on paper.

To my Love, my Life, my Inspiration…you infuse me with your radiant touch;

My dear Vishal Persaud,
I love you.

Moonlight Purlieu

Meet me under the moonlight purlieu
In the middle of the night as stars secure the sapphire sky.
Take my hand and lead the way,
Let us circle the moon's edge
And wander to a place that we know.
Enchant me beneath the starlit sky,
Touch my skin with your seductive glance
And carry me with you under the still aurora-
Of this dear summer's night;
Entice me, confine me,
As florets blossom vibrant colors,
Enjoin me to walk with you upon the steamy
Sand of a dusky shore;
And as the sun is starting to peek through the evident sky,
Come with me, enthrall me, and sing to me.
Serenade me with a song and put me to sleep,
Find a pattern within the rhythms of my heartbeat
And make me yours all over again.
Collide with me under the moonlight mile
In the core of the night,
Speak to me with your lenient voice,
Exhale with me, make me yours-
Day after day.

Ocean's Blue

You are indeed my first drop of rain,
my orange crystal gem that sparkles
upon me under the moonlit night.
Your eyes tell a secret tale to my silent mind,
you are sending me a signal
as my heart clings to yours and
we meet once again
under the plastered blanket of stars.
Together we flow with the emerald waters,
we sail east and leave all behind
as we become one with the soothing breeze,
Calming and captivating.
Your kisses are like luscious raindrops
that melt upon me.
You dissolve in my heart as your scents
haunt my skin on this peaceful evening.
I bring myself closer to you,
Your subtle skin whispers to me as
The silver rain falls upon us
In the quiet hours of a rapid Sunday night,
And we float,
Holding on to each other as we sail
On the beauty of the ocean's blue.

Our Song

We fade into the night
with soothing lyrics from a peaceful song.
Your lips never looked more luscious
and your eyes never reflected so bright
upon me as we dance under the moonlight.

I am touched by the scents of you,
and a warm magnetic feeling deep inside
is pulling me closer and closer where
our hearts begin to beat together
as we waltz beneath the vivid sky.

A reverie is taking place nearby,
there is an aurora touching the stems
of each rose bush beneath our feet,
and suddenly, the stars are starting to dance
with the softness of our song.

And we remain enchanting,
Close by, around, and within each other.
Your beauteous vanity spark upon me
as we drift closer to the edge of the ocean
to be captivated by the only passionate wave.

The song is reaching its final verse and
your eyes are starting to dim.
Our heartbeats begin to suspend,
we hold on to what is around and within us
as dusk is starting to cover our grounds.

Debbie

Her lonely tears flowed
with anguished pain,
as her escape seemed
Mediocre to the world.
Cries from inside pulled
back the emotions
and made her accept death
like a helpless child.
The air, scented with hatred,
Fears, and anger somehow
Managed to slip,
While her beauty started to
Disappear every minute until
The excruciating pain from the
Last bullet hit the center of her
Broken heart,
Shattering every part of it.
Hours after, her blood covered the floor,
Hair fallen on her face,
Almost as if she was asleep,
on the very bottom of the staircase
Where she was found dead
on that agonizing day.

Lenient Glow

As I lay my dreams on scarlet petals,
I hum to the enthralling song divulging
through my ears on a blissful evening.

I hold on close to childhood memories,
Encircled with eloquent passion,
enough to last a lifetime, locked within me.

I am waiting for the sun to fall beneath the sky,
when the moon comes out and whisper to me
as I furl my wings and radiate with its beam.

The wind seems like an enigma,
sweetly colliding on my skin, serenading me,
making an apt for solace.

My heart cadences with the rhythm of an entrancing tune
and I dance with the sounds of a wave that is
visiting the shore, conceiving music for my soul.

Inside, I am smiling a thousand smiles,
I am gleaming with the blue sparks from the ocean
as a new feeling is being composed deep inside.

I joyfully pick up the pieces of my reveries
between the stars and pack them away within
the palm of my hands.

Night is visiting and I must leave for now,
and return again tomorrow when the sun is falling asleep,
kissing me with its lenient golden glows.

Invaded

I hear an eerie mournful sound,
it came from above.
I turned to look and saw a shooting star
Disappearing from my sight.
I find myself crumbling to the ground
as I am poisoned
and no longer have the
will to move.
I have been cursed by the devil in you;
the darkness within your eyes
has slashed my veins
and left the blood to drip on my broken dreams.
There is a little place inside of me
where I would escape to
but somehow you have invaded me,
leaving no peace in my once gleaming
world filled with sunlight.

Imprints

We've set sail on these frosty waves before.
I see familiar ships with nets and anchors
Swaying in the misty blue of the capricious ocean.
With granted dreams unlocked, dripping
in the already scented water from
the gleaming brine embraced by the moon's
Beam from all feasible corners.
We make our way to shore,
quavering on familiar trails left the night before.
For a moment,
I was lost within the raptures of him.
Our skin touched and it was magical,
we created a storm that pushed
Raindrops through the miraculous sky,
while in his eyes I found beauteous trace
of his love for me.
The rain showers her beauty upon the already wet sand
Forming imprints as we sift though the minutes
Looking for clues towards our destination unknown.

Radiant

It's difficult to formulate a poem for you.
I can never determine the words to elaborate the verse,
the flow would somehow be off,
and the imagery would be imperfect.
For you are too sublime to write about.
I would sit here for hours and try to find radiant
Things to say but in the end,
there is no poem, or no song, or no verse that
can ever divulge your tale.
You are quite a man that when you are around,
I am at my best; your laughter enlightens my world.
Your smile encircles me with joy.
Your angelic face is too precious to write about,
there would be no realistic word to do virtue
to such a man, standing in front of me.
Your hands are the best I have ever seen,
I cannot find the right words to put on paper
To describe them.
You are merely divine in my eyes and whatever
I compose for you, whether a poem or a song,
it should be exuding with liquid gold,
and the words should somehow be diffused with
the dust from the wings of a butterfly.
And the pen, that mighty pen should be ignited
by the brightest colors of a rainbow,
Settling across the sky on a Sunday evening.
That my dear is the only way I can write an epic
about this divine man, standing near me.
Until then, please endure these words.
Until I can give you a poem radiating with gold,
Written by a pen embraced by a rainbow,
please accept this verse for it is all I can present to you
at the moment.

Dear Daddy

All I have left of you
Is a black and white picture,
Vintage collection,
Chipped in the corners
And curled up edges, locked away
In my scrapbook;
With a scent of rose petals.
My notions of you are radiant and lifting,
never a dull avail, knowing that I originated
from such vanity and grandeur.
I picture your smiles to be
the most subdued of all,
like the falling of the sun into
the extremities of the ocean.
I envision your voice to be
Ardent and wistful,
caressing the words as you speak.
In my black and white image of you,
The sun is reflecting off the softness of your hair
And the resoluteness of you
Quite enthralling each time
I look at you knowing that I am your creation,
And from your lineage, my heart found its beat.
Anyone can be a father,
but it takes an exceptional man to be a daddy,
and whether you are with me or not
it suits me perfectly acknowledging that
I am the child whose smiles made you content.

Pain

Suddenly, it was the break of day.
I waited patiently for the sun to come up,
All night long, thoughts of swimming in a
River with no will to swim crossed my mind,
And I couldn't help but to let go of whatever
Faith I had tucked away inside
As a silent pain crawled within,
Bringing tears to my eyes, once again.
You pretend to know nothing about the ache
You have left beneath my skin,
It is almost like you don't notice my cries,
Especially when I am all alone,
Left to suffer from the horrid memories you have
Created with your actions.
You have poisoned the air I breathe
with your filth and anger;
I find it difficult to sleep because
Of haunting dreams.
The sun is beginning to peek through
the creases of my unlocked door,
and yet, sleep hasn't welcomed me.
It's Sunday, and the world will lay back
and whisper sweet songs with the western wind,
as I sit down, all alone, thinking of the pain
you have left in the center of my stomach.

A Childhood Memory

We walk down the sidewalks on Amethyst Street,
Making our way to paradise's door.
The sun is beaming through the stillness of the trees
that stands above,
covering the steaming floor below.
Laughter comes from everywhere as we attempt to
Pick flower buds and place them in our hair,
Beautifully grasping a piece of childhood
To take with us forever.
I look up, accepting every ray of light
Directing towards my face,
Memorable and sudden,
my tiny heart pounds more and more
with unknown excitement as our adventure
becomes a fairytale.
Rose bushes and white swings on the way,
with a trail to heaven's door,
awaiting us as we glide through the misty heat
Of an alluring day.
We reach our destination,
Soothing kisses from aromas of flowers,
Swimming in the air
and we mark a spot,
Building a seat on the grass and wait for the sun to go down.
Soon enough, evening will come
and the City below will light up,
forming a galaxy of stars,
like a blanket, calming our dreamy souls.

Eventide

I stay awake just to see you sleep,
I conform myself closer to ascertain
the rhythms of your heart
as nightfall encircles the evening.
And as you begin to suspire a dream,
I huddle my wings and fly away with you,
into a land where we encounter each eventide.
We settle at the edge of the moon,
overlooking the emerald sea,
splurging against shore and
waking every living creature nearby.
We whirl through thin air,
Becoming one with the sky
as we tiptoe between each alluring star,
Etching our names as we go by.
We finally attain an enchanting wave,
Rushing along the ocean's surface
As we sail along,
Washing away our thoughts
Within the misty blue,
We approach closer to the rising
Of the golden celestial,
Inevitably showering her beauty
Upon the lustrous waters,
Soothing us on a vivid wave,
Sailing away…

Summer

The golden sunlight today tells me
that Spring is right around the corner,
The fresh green grass, growing, almost covering
sleepy sidewalks reminds of the warm days
When aroma of flowers circles the air.
The gentle breeze today tells me of a summer
that we are about to have only months to come.
The mild days ahead are somewhat promising,
Filled with luscious memories to last a lifetime...
The stars tonight seems lenient and still,
Covering the sky with sparkles,
Adding a smile on my face each time I look up.
The winter night leaves me with thoughts
that Summer is only a few tomorrows away
and in no time,
The streets will be covers with scents of fresh cut grass...
Rosebuds will spring their beauty from every direction,
Painting a picture with their colors.
This cold and horrid night gives me hopes
of the summer we are about to have.
Only a few months from now we will be covered
with warmth...the golden sun will become orange...
Embracing the surface with happiness.

Edge of the moon

Loving you is like seeing the sunshine
After a month long rainfall,
Loving you is like floating on a crimson wave
In the middle of Summer,
When the sun reaches down
To kiss the surface of the earth,
Leaving everything with a touch of gold.
Loving you like seeing
the western wind making love to the branches
of a tiresome tree in the middle of the day.
Seeing your smile is like sitting at the edge of the moon
and looking down at the world below.
Being with you is like circling the stars in the middle
Of a dark, yet peaceful night. Holding you near is like caressing
the first wave that hits the shore
on a warm Sunday afternoon.
Loving you is like walking a mile long
Just to see a colorful rainbow
in the end.
It's like being embraced by the morning sun,
Put to sleep by the beauty of the evening...
And cascaded by the eruptions of the night's delight.

Elaine Colgrave

Writing, to me is a Godsend in so many ways. I have had a very turbulent life but I will not dwell on that or tomorrow may as well never come again. For the most part my turbulence has brought me power.

I gained momentum and strength through the power to forgive; yet I have a memory like an elephant. A gentle person, a romantic at heart, strong and confident with my children as they see me as their rock and so they should.

Born in England, I was brought to Australia when I was 18mths old and grew up in a small country town. I moved to the city with my children and my life was renewed and once again began to write.
Writing is the ultimate way to get to know oneself through sharing innermost dreams, thoughts, realities, wishes, hopes and fantasies. This is who I am, what I do and what has made me the person that I am today.

I was still chasing rainbows hoping to meet my soul mate until I met my partner Rob, now I am getting closer to finding me.

No surprises, what you see and what you read is what you get…Simply Lainee.

Poetry to Me

Those quiet moments in time day or night
When all in an instant seems to feel right,
Images, feelings, a sight to behold;
Poetry to me is worth more than gold.

When sun kisses sea and sky touches land
Elusive as dreams out of reach by hand,
a tear caught in time, a smile stretching far,
Words stirring feelings wherever you are.

Fantasies captured or expanded facts,
harsh realizations or simple kind acts,
a reflection of life from yesterday,
hope for tomorrow envisioned today.

The knowing, stirring, beginning or end,
The face of a stranger, the love of a friend,
The moon shining brightly lighting the way,
The stars in the night sky which frolic and play.

A sunset, a whisper, a rainbow on high,
Passion and pleasure, a laugh or a sigh,
Clouds changing shape, shadows dancing around,
Vision, an emotion, a touch or a sound.

Sudden inspirations, memories too,
Actions, inflictions and natural hue,
Thoughts lay unspoken, untold or unsaid,
Written on impulse and penned to be read.

Life, love and loss, realistic or surreal,
Guiding the soul and the spirit to feel,
Happiness, sadness, elation or cold,
in any genre poetry is gold.

Alone (I'm an Island)

It's coming in waves; first tears then pain;
'til numbness settles back in again.

Your smile, your eyes, your laughter, your face,
your shadow drifts all around this place.

My life between each heartbeat
felt safe, secure, felt strong, felt sweet.

The taste of love, which fed my soul,
felt complete and real, felt good, felt whole.

Now the void of losing you,
of losing my grasp on a dream come true.

Feels weird, feels wrong, feels strange, feels blue,
deep in my soul I'm still loving you.

Alone I'm an island surrounded by sea
lost in an ocean that's too big for me.

At Peace

Watching the water ebb then fall
stealing the sand between my toes,
I ponder pages of my life:
where the final chapter flows.

With towel-wrap I keep at bay
the shivering, which lingers on,
so tired from swimming currents deep
I watch the sand I stand upon.

Disappearing beneath my weight
like hours as they seem to fly,
another day has come and gone
As sun sinks low from orange sky.

Highlighting green in nearby trees
the sunset forms their silhouette,
a memory instilled inside;
a wondrous sight I'll not forget.

The stillness sets with silent thoughts
As shades of pink disturb the blue,
One thing's for certain; this I know:
My life begins and ends with you.

Arousal

Arousal's wrought;
outside of dreams
it shines in shades
from golden beams
of sun so bright
in splattered rays
enhancing life
in new-born days.

Spilling forth
through sky and sea
to cleanse the soul;
so spirit is free
alluring life
for you and me
with natural essence;
complacently.

Grasses green
when newly mown
through little seeds
rebirth is sown
freshness inhaled
upon the breeze
scented in the
nearby trees.

Rain falls light
by day, by night,
from clouded grey
loom pillows to sight
leaving a misty
haze unseen
as sunlight splashes
upon evergreen.

Wondrous riches;
a simple fair
sought and found
most everywhere
gifts of life
for you, for me,
given everyday;
complacently.

A world of rays
by day, by night
to give us
everlasting light
by sun, through stars,
by earth and sea
we take for granted
naturally.

Perfect Day

Mellow sunlight
Pale blue dawn
Glisten gently
Early morn
Budding flowers
Swaying trees
Whisper softly
Subtle breeze

Kiss away
Yawns of sleep
Fading dreams
Not ours to keep
Shine on new day
Souls arise
Wiping the sleep
From weary eyes

Stretch and breathe
Crisp morning air
Welcome life
Without a care
Feel the vibrance
Flow anew
A perfect day
To wake up to!

If Confidence Falters

It's hard to meet one face to face
or look another in the eye,
to find your place; your comfort space,
when confidence has said goodbye.

You reach for stars not there at night
then lose the hope brought forth by light,
when darkness calls and silence falls
And all your dreams drop out of sight.

You swim upstream against the tide
as pressure mounts and sadness rules,
Frustrations rise within the guise
of paranoia cast by fools.

Just take a look inside your soul
You'll find there is no need to hide,
In times of doubt get up and shout,
Release the fear pent up inside.

Don't let another bring you down
Or tell you you're incompetent,
In all you do be true to you;
Remember you are heaven sent.

Moments Like These

As I watched you sleeping,
dreaming in our bed;
your smile spread with your whisper,
And my name, is all you said.
Such love shown in a moment,
making me so aware,
A little voice inside me sang
a song of thanks and prayer.

It's moments like these
which turn memories
into diamonds shining bright,
through love that's found
as facets abound,
in endless shades of light.

There's so much understanding
when my words go unsaid,
So much depth and meaning
when my mind's not easily read.
There's so much found
between the lines,
it's showing everywhere;
I love the way you know me;
it shows how much you care.

And I think you are truly beautiful,
you shine like a diamond bright,
you're the memory
which will carry me,
forever towards the light.
Your love and understanding
with depth and meaning through,
your facets are found
in the love all around,
in the moments I spend with you.

Perhaps one day I will tell you
Just how I feel inside,
I'll say the words left unspoken;
I won't be afraid
And I won't hide,
I'll offer you a memory
And my diamond too,
Will shine bright,
With love which is found
As new facets abound,
In endless shades of light.

Yes, it's moments like these
which turn memories
into diamonds shining bright,
through love which is found
as new facets abound,
in endless shades of light.

The Power of Ra

I stand
stripped naked
with arms outstretched
totally succumbing
to the magnificence
of one so powerful
in sheer and absolute
abandonment

Your warmth
washes over me
bathing my body
cleansing my mind
releasing my soul
as the ever-empowering
beauty of your light
reflects prisms
of joyous shades
off the normally inane
bringing all to life
once more

Enchantment
dances around me
cast once more
by your natural charisma
easing my mind
devouring all insecurities
and inner fears
as the gift of a new day
is born

The ever-changing
aquamarine
beckons to me
beneath your power
and my guard is released
as I wander silently
into the ocean of life
a slave to your
magnetic allure
almighty Ra

While You Were Sleeping

As I stare upon your
silhouette
moonlight's silver stream
sends a perfect outline around
your
softly sculpted little face
casting a gentle glow
through the
bedroom window
to enchant your dreams
as you sleep unaware
of the beauty found in this moment

With your tiny hand
tucked under your
cheekand your little nose
shining in the moonlight
my heart skips a
beat
knowing you are here with me
and I watch your chest rise and fall
as I gently place the baby blanket
over your pyjamas

as I kiss you lightly the crystal sun catcher
hanging from the nursery window
tinkles in the whispering breeze
and I smile as I remember
the day
we decorated your bedroom

Then with charcoal in hand
I once again begin to sketch
another precious memory
Into my keeper of dreams.

Sadness Reigns

Sadness reigns in solemn hue
Between the depth of black and blue,
Sun bows down to moonlight's glow
As restless thoughts begin to grow.

Casting shadows; web complete,
A doubting mind begins retreat.
Hiding beneath a palisade,
Burning bridges before they're made.

Protecting self; subconscious rules,
Enamoured past deceives all fools
As sun outshines the fading moon,
Predestined paths unwind too soon.

New day calls in shades so bright,
Mindless thoughts ebb with the night.
Life sings songs in harmony,
Awakening joy to set souls free.

Misgivings pass; eclipsed once more
As beauty shines on golden shore.
Life goes on; the waves resound,
Ghost's of past no longer found.

Alone (With Midnight)

My mind's at one with nightfall
lost in midnight so serene,
walking barefoot in the backyard
over dewdrop-coated green.

A solitary star shines bright;
I smile and sigh then quietly yawn,
watching the stream of burning light
as starlight glitters across my lawn.

This wondrous night will never end;
it floats across the sky to you,
at peace with self I comprehend
why dawn returns to me anew.

Quietly closing the outside door
I slide into my bed to sleep,
leaving solace to fade once more;
I dream 'til dawn in slumber deep.

Caught (In Dreams)

I'm caught in streams
Of endless dreams
Feeling down in my heart
Awaiting the point
When life will anoint
The blessing of peace; torn apart

Enchantment has ceased
Yet thoughts have increased
They're slowly driving me mad
Sleep slides away
As night turns to day
Still I don't know why I'm sad

It's crazy I know
Just goes to show
We all have our days without sun
The moon and the stars
Are as distant as Mars
When life is devoid of all fun

Utopia teases
As anger releases
Pent up distress from inside
With floodgates now open
And feelings outspoken
My happiness won't be denied

I choose joy over pain
And relinquish the stain
Laying waste on my mind for so long
I'll turn life around
Sing again to the sound
And get back to where I belong

Lost in dreams
And endless streams
Of fantasy rides in the skies
To swim in the sea
Chasing harmony
And spark a new light in my eyes.

Chasing Trust

Chasing Trust.
Touch me softly
Love me gently
Your world is new to me
Soothing my mind
Erasing my doubts
Slowly setting me free
Taking your time
By taking mine
Teaching me liberty
Guide me well
With careful steps
Towards the real me
Giving me time
To know your mind
To delve inside and see
If your ways
And the life you lead
Is what I want for me
With a gentle hand
Firmly stand
I'll follow if you lead
No promises shared
Nor guarantees
Mean we will succeed
I'll give us a go
If you journey slow
It's all I really need
To trust in you
In all you do
To live the life I heed

Break down the walls
My stumbles and falls
Catch me if you can
Until I believe
Each time you leave
You really are a gentle man

Color Red

Waking up
to the clatter and bang
of your bad temper
and noisy attempts
to make my life
even more uncomfortable
than it has been
so far lately

I close my eyes
and play possum
as your war drum
beats loudly

expressed in everything
you touch
pick up then drop
or slam down
with vehemence

as if these inane objects
will bring an avenue of relief
to your all consuming hate

break a plate
and let it all out
so we can return
once more
to the place where
we began
before this side
of your personality surfaced

because I am not your enemy

the choices you made
were your own
and I refuse to wear
the color red.

Giving (Me Life)

You come to me
like a dream in the night
and enter my soul
with your guiding light
bringing relief
when needed so much
to a heavy heart
as whispered tears clutch
for enlightenment
of body and soul
willing me well
once again to be whole

You come to me
like a dream in the night
and give of your soul
depleting your light
helping me breathe
holding my hand
showing in your heart
you understand
feeling my pain
with every heart beat
warming me gently
with your body heat

You come to me
like a knight in my dream
and capture my heart
within every scene
'til breathing comes easy
and heartbeat regains
as strength is returned
and your love remains
deep in my soul
written on my mind
shining forever
so tender and kind.

In Constance Rise

May loving hearts in constance rise
With feelings deep in mystic eyes
And roses bud with petals fair
As sunlight dances in the air

Spirits float with weightlessness
Minds released from all duress
Tummy spins in pirouette
Lips brush lips; never to forget

Kiss, first kiss; anticipated
Dreams, all dreams; now satiated
Same old, same old; appears anew
Velvet touch like morning dew

Glowing cheeks are roses red
Euphoria grows through words unsaid
Blessings sent from up above
You're never too old to fall in love

In the Morrow

I'll love you in the morrow
Till our dreams we bid adieu,
And sunlight shines away the mist
As dawn arises new,
For love within the morrow's
A hypnotic place to steal;
The time between the pulse of life
Where souls are sent to heal.

I'll hold you in the morrow
Till the day retreats to night,
Where every star's a signature
Of true love's sacred plight.
You'll leave me in the morrow:
A spirit illuming death,
As sunlight shines away the mist
And heightens ev'ry breath.

To love me in the morrow
Where dreams aren't out of reach,
Are times between the pulse of life
When conscious minds beseech.
As the wind blows through the morrow
Aurora sings her song,
With time I hope the morrow
Brings you back where you belong.

Migraine

Like thunder
in a sudden storm
you arrive
with debilitating vengeance
stealing mobility
controlling freedom
to set about
destroying
all I have taken for granted
in everyday life

You sabotage
perfectly laid out plans
with brutality
condemning me
to torture and duress
for days on end
stealing all thoughts
enveloping my world
turning me into an invalid
blurring my vision
and stealing sight
as muscles tighten
agony arises

Then as quickly as
the sudden storm
and thunder arrived
you dissipate
everything I lost
is returned once more
leaving a path
of unfulfilled obligations behind
with the trail of neglect
the only proof
you ever existed.

River Dawn

Reflections in the early dawn
Filled with promise so crystal clear
As time stands still 'pon river at morn
Last shades of darkness disappear
Glass top throws back all cast upon
Outlined trees; rocks silhouette
Bring promise for the new day born
Float slow in stillness so perfect
A memory seen not to forget
I stand and watch and you are near
As sun sits low unrisen yet
So thankful now that I am here
To look upon the river glass
Seeing reflections on the face
Of water in mountain retreat
Witness paradise in this place.

Sweet Sunrise

As sunrise spills across the dawn
in orange hue and pink bouquet,
upon the sands in early morn
I witness beauty on this day.

Reflected off the mirrored blue
of azure sky and aqua sea,
the sailor's song rings out so true
as streaks of red bring luck to me.

A purple haze within the mist
Contours the spectral of display,
as peace of mind serenely sought
tenfold has dealt supreme array.

Upon these sands I sit in awe
and watch the day begin anew,
as rainbows filter on the shore
and brightly shine in morning dew.

Rose Freeman

I am South African and live in the beautiful Cape, in the shade of Table Mountain. Most of my poetry I write in the dark nights of my soul. It speaks of the illusionary perfect love we all yearn for. I am a published writer.

Winter

The leaves have rusted
On the vine
And the oaks have shed
Their golden cloaks

Hope lies bleak
In my reason
And the north wind
Whistles through the willow
Cutting cold
Like the blade
Of the knife
Wedged in my heart

Still

When I think about you
I realize that I never did love your tranquility
Your ability to say nothing
To me it seemed more like a dark-eyed vigilance
Then one day, with nothing said, you were gone
Left, as silently as you had come
Though I no longer look for reasons to beat up on myself,
I am in mourning for my wasted years
Now, although I think I love you still
I can look in the mirror and see
I look better when I am not wearing you

Colors of the Day

From my porch
I watch another orange sun
rise in the sky
as I sip my early
morning tea

I wonder
at the colors of the day
and breathe in
the giddy scent of the
'yesterday, today
and tomorrow' tree

Thoughts of you
drift through my mind
and then I realize
I can no more remember
the color of
your lying eyes

When You Miss Me at Christmas

You will have a picture in your mind
of where I am and what I will be doing
on Christmas day.
You will be sad.
This I know.
Maybe you'll miss the ritual
you came to know over the years,
and the friends and family who cared.

The memory will make you still.

I will not be thinking of you.
I will be sitting beside a fir tree
brought down from the mountains,
reading good wishes and accepting gifts
given with joy and love.

I will not mention your name
or wonder where you are.
I have decided that you will not
live in my head anymore without paying rent.

Just a Woman

For all the days
Of amity
I spent as many nights
Alone
For all the nights
Of rapture
I spent as many days
In sorrow
I've refuted my God
While mourning my dead
Feigned innocence
While telling a lie
I've wept for one man
And loved another
To destruction
I've broken a promise
And a heart or two
I've stayed for the win
Left for the loss
Rolled the dice
And started all over again
But, never for one moment
Have I wished to be
Someone else
For I have cradled
The seed of my womb
Embraced unconditional love
And seen hope in the dawning
Of each new day

When Time Kicked In

You were gone
So I filled
The empty shape of you
With scents remembered,
Promises spoken,
And hope for yesterday's dreams
To come true
I wore
Your daytime shadow
And in my room
At night
Your dark patch
Upon the wall
Then one day
With time
The sun came shining through
And when I turned
Myself around
The shadow of you
Was nowhere to be found

Alienated

At the end of the day
when light fades away
and darkness closes in
do you dream of a place
left far behind,
where love, laughter and plenty
came easy?

When the sun doesn't shine
and life is unkind
can you keep me
from your mind?

Villanelle for Gregory

Child of my spirit, patience, I implore
The woe of life and death we do endure
Born from my womb, I could not love you more
Not all our dreams will have an open door
And passing time does bring its magic cure
Child of my spirit, patience, I implore
To chattels of this world we cannot claw
And all good men fall prey to wrongful lure
Born from my womb, I could not love you more
Sometimes, we will not pull the longest straw
And good intent can't shield a heart tho' pure
Child of my spirit, patience, I implore
To ride the wind, the storm must come before
And death will come to claim us all, for sure
Born from my womb, I could not love you more
Consider, all your schemes will have a flaw
And to your fears you will become inure
Child of my spirit, patience, I implore
Born from my womb, I could not love you more

Don't Wait for the Fall

Should you come home
to me, in November,
the soft rains of autumn
would have cooled the air,
the last rose of summer
spilled her worth,
and the falling leaves
laid a rusted carpet
upon the earth.

Warmth will be gone
from the noonday sun,
swallow birds
flown without warning,
and the dark of night
would linger too long
before morning,
should you come home
to me, in November.

No Closure

Why you left me
I don't need to know
I don't care now
Where you had to go

I never wonder
Where you lay your head
Or if there's someone
Asleep in your bed

I have no concern
If you're happy or sad
Whether your life's been
For the good or bad

Too many years
Have passed us by
And the river I cried
Has long run dry

But all my days
I'll wonder why
You could not stop
To tell me goodbye

Pensive

Sometimes when I look to the setting sun
Awaiting dark to take the light away
I mourn the fading of another day
And wonder when my time to die will come

Long years spilled, the joy has just begun
And death would be inopportune array
So much to write so many words to say
Where do old poets go when day is done

For dreams untold and amnesty not shown
Will time allow for new thought and amends
Or will I need to spend these days alone
And not go on to where the next road bends

To suck the marrow from contention's bone
I need more time before this short life ends

Regret

Words
From you
Stab my heart
And pluck at
Twisted threads
Of hurt
And anger
Binding a wound
So deep

It is the falsity
I can't endure
The spewing
Of poison
From your mouth
While the grief
Of your self
Betrayal
Echoes
In your eyes

Endless

Endless
The days of joy
I found within your smile
Then one sad day you went your way
Severed sweet dreams to still the wanderlust
A raging battle deep inside
Pride did not beg you stay
And days remain
Endless

First Love

Come sing a song of days long gone
A sweet refrain of callow love
The foolishness when two lips meet
With promises that love will last
The magic of a harvest moon
And the splendor of the night star

Let's wish upon the evening star
For all our hope can not be gone
There is still splendor in the moon
And promise of enduring love
The magic of a dream can last
And sweet true love we still may meet

O' my true love when shall we meet
And look upon the evening star
With promises that dreams will last
Long after days of youth are gone
Together we can dream this love
And bask in the light of the moon

I gaze up at the harvest moon
And dream of when our lips shall meet
With promises of truest love
Wish granted by the evening star
And when I think all hope is gone
I will the magic night to last

For all sweet dreams of love to last
And shine as brightly as the moon
I need to let my fears be gone
The chance that we will never meet
For when I wished upon that star
I wished for you to be my love

Love of my life, my callow love
I made-believe this love would last
I wished upon the evening star
Spent hours gazing at the moon
Longing for us, once more to meet
Before the days of youth are gone

Come sing of love and shining moon
Of dreams that last and hearts that meet
See the night star, hope is not gone

Sunburnt

The air is still
A misty haze
Rises shimmering
From the tar

Oak-lined sidewalks
Lend little shade
From the midday sun

In the valley
The willow hangs limp
Over the bank
Of a dried-up stream

The herd lies down
In the field
And the robin
Waits for night
To sing

Sundown
Brings no respite
The maddening chirp
Of the cricket
Persists into the heat
Of the night

The earth barely cools
In the hour before dawn
And the sun rises
With a vengeance
When summer comes
To Africa

The Cooling-Off Period

I had my heart broken
Once
Long time ago
By an adulterous leech
Who left me
High and dry
Now
Although
I can't seem to fit
The pieces
Back together
I am told
Time will heal
So
I am just
Hanging around
Being real cool
And waiting
For this time thing
To kick in

September

September,
And the sun
Begins to linger in the sky
Bringing warmth
And warning
Of the blistering summer days
To come
Trees boast with blossoms
Of pink and white
And the air is heavy
With the scent of jasmine in bloom
Oaks cover their branches
In varied shades of green
And the " chor- chor" song
Of returning swallows
Can be heard
Long after twilight
Away from Africa
I would surely wither and die
Like the wild arum
In a summer 'vlei'

Everywhere I Go

This morning I stopped by Pick 'n Pay to buy two onions,
the Job Finder, a packet of smokes
and a pre-packed dinner for one.

Somebody's short, fat grandmother, chewing gum
and wearing one of those ridiculous chef hats,
tried to push a packet of curried chicken sosaties my way.

In a senior moment,
I told her that my husband did not eat chicken.

Then I needed to buy a slab of chocolate to feed
the butterflies fluttering around inside me.

I went home.

It beats me as to why they play sad love songs
in supermarkets on Saturday mornings.

Deserted

I can't see tomorrow
From this island
Where you left me
The horizon is obscured
By low- hanging
Morning mists
And at night
Dark clouds
Hide the stars
And the moon
It is of no use
To hope
There is no help
For me
And I wonder
Has rescue come
To your island

I Still Dream of You

We've spent our youth, the innocence is lost,
swept far away upon the wings of time.
The piper paid, we pause to count the cost
of off-beam choices that we held sublime.
Now days are short and seem to hurry by,
the coming night cannot be kept at bay.
It is no use to question, wonder why
we lost this love somewhere along the way.
But when I dream, I only dream of you,
a place where my sweet memories abide,
for in my heart I think I always knew
you would not be forever by my side.
Though I will never touch your face again
I'll sing deep in my heart love's sweet refrain.

And now the days just seem to hurry by

To me you've always been a brother true
a place where my sweet memories are found
and when my days of darkness made me blue
I knew that you'd make the time to come around

To me you've been a brother fair and true
A place where youth's sweet memories abound
Like in the very heart of you Found

Through all the years I held you by my side
and you have always been a brother true
A place where my sweet memories abide
held in the of you
To me you've been a brother fair and true
And held the lamp so I could see the way

To me you'll always be
The best
A place where my
sweet mem'ries rest

Where you dug in
And stood your ground
And now that we are growing old

Ron Howard

I have been writing poetry for over twenty years mostly for my own edification, but I would occasionally share my work with close friends. A little over a year ago I was accepted to publish my collection, which I titled " A Search for Meaning". It has been and adventure and opened me up to a whole new world of possibilities that I had never even considered. Since publishing my work it has forced me to take my poetry a lot more seriously. I have spent a lot of time trying to hone my craft and feel that I am becoming a better poet and writer with each passing day. I have a long way to go, but it is the journey after all that makes life worth living. In addition to writing I have also been developing new poetry sites in an effort to help expand the reach of poets and poetry to the world.

The first is Poetry in the Park. (http://www.freewebs.com/poetry_in_the_park) This site has been developed as a resource for poets and has over 800 links to other poetry and writing related sites, articles, and poetry.

The other is a poetry forum (http://poetryinthepark.proboards59.com/index.cgi) it is a meeting place for poets and those who love poetry. It was created to provide a safe and comfortable place for poets to meet and share their ideas, poetry and just to unwind. It was this group that inspired this book and it is my hope that you will enjoy your time in the park.

Searching for Beth

The sun was shining bright that day
As parents laughed and children played.

Out on the beach just having some fun
Peacefully baking under the sun.

A well deserved rest, my soul to recharge
No worries, no cares, no debts looming large.

Away from the hustle and bustle of life
Away from my job and all of its strife.

Across the world with my kid and my wife
Enjoying our time in this island paradise.

Under blue skies and bright shinning sun
My worst nightmare had just begun.

It came from the sea in a foaming white wall
Which came crashing down on top of us all.

A panic ensued and we struggled to flee
But most were caught up and swept out to sea

I frantically searched and was unable to see
My wife or my daughter as I clung to a tree.

The waves rushed by as I clung to that branch
For thousands of others they hadn't a chance.

For hours and hours, clinging for life
Desperately searching for signs of my wife.

At long last the water began to recede
I came down from my perch and fell to my knees

Battered and bruised in my exhaustive state
I wept uncontrollably as I pondered their fate

My heart full of pain and feeling confused
I walked through the rubble searching for clues

Hoping to find them safe and alive
Praying that they had also survived

I walked along streets filled with debris
Wanting so much their faces to see.

Then my heart fell and I started to weep
As I looked down at her there at my feet.

The woman I love with all of my heart
Was lying there lifeless. My world fell apart.

How could this happen? Where'd I go wrong?
How come I'm still breathing, when with her I belong?

Gathering what strength I had left
I rose to my feet and kept searching for Beth.

My sweet little angel, my daughter of five
Is there any hope that she's still alive?

Searching for hours, nearly dead on my feet
I see a small child cloaked in a sheet.

I slowly kneel down and pull back this shroud
And when I do see her I cry out aloud.

My life is now over, I give it away.
God take me with them. I don't want to stay.

You Say You Love Me

How can you say you love me
When you know not what it means
To love another with all your heart
And care about their dreams.

You cannot say you love me
When you turn and walk away
Just because we argue
And things don't go your way.

You cannot say you care
About all the things I dream
When all you have to say
Comes no softer than a scream.

When I can't remember
Hearing kind words from you
That is when I know for certain
That all we had is through.

My Angel

Oh, my heart weighs heavy
on this cold, winters eve
for my special angel
this life she had to leave.

On this earthly journey
she had always been my guide
and if I ever stood in need
she was right there by my side.

Her love would draw you in
like the moth goes to the flame.
I'm sure that life with out her
will never be the same.

Practicing the word
sent down from God above
to treat every person
with tenderness and love.

She was my example
and taught me to see
how to live this life
the way it was meant to be.

I Fight For...

I stare into the emptiness
of this dark, dismal night
and contemplate the reasons
I have come here to fight.

I've gone across the ocean
leaving all I know behind
to help protect the freedoms
endowed to all mankind.

I do not fight for oil
no matter what they say.
I came to fight for freedom
and the American way.

I fight for my family
my children and my wife.
I fight for neighbors
to preserve their way of life.

I fight for the dream
of what we all could be
if the people of this world
were granted liberty.

Boredom

The silence is deafening
in this small lonely space
as I sit and I ponder
this burden I face.

Alone in the dark
no signs of reprieve
from madness that enters
my mind on this eve.

The darkness surrounds me
in a cold, dark embrace
and chokes out all hope
that I'll soon leave this place

Moist Pleasure

I see you lying there before me.
A steam-filled invitation to partake of your wonders.
The scent of lavender fills the air
as I move closer to you.

Your soothing touch beckons me.

Slowly,

I remove this armor.

Piece by piece.

Until I stand,
cold and naked before you.

Gently,
I slip between your walls.
You cover me completely
in a warm blanket of moist pleasure.

My breath is taken away.

In a euphoric state I lay,
submerged in your warm embrace.
Tensions are released
and I lose consciousness.

I awake to find
what was once warm and inviting,
has now turned cold and damp.
My wrinkled skin
is now a testament
to my long slumber.

Slowly, I rise.

Taking my leave from you
I wrap my nakedness
in the comfort of a soft towel.

As I leave behind
this porcelain paradise.

My Father the Soldier

He's gone to fight the evil
to keep me safe at home.
He's gone to serve his country
and left me all alone.

We miss him very much
and pray for him each night.
We hope that he'll be safe
as he battles for the right.

Freedom is not given
it comes at a great cost.
Not counted by the dollars spent,
but by the lives we've lost.

I'm proud that he was willing
to go and do his part.
I'm glad that he's my father
whom I love with all my heart.

Daydreams

I slumber not, yet still I dream
as thoughts of you prevail.
Your beauty haunts my mind
and on my heart assails.

Those sapphire pools draw me in
to drown me in thy gaze
and shroud my heart completely
in a ward and loving haze.

The memories of your touch
ignite the fires within
while the taste still lingers
from your alabaster skin.

The passion that we shared
I keep forever in my heart
and think about you often
when we are far apart.

Pure Love

As a boy of four
I seldom have a care,
but I had to notice
my neighbor sitting there.

On his porch he sat
in silent disbelief
unable to control
or even hide his grief.

Tears ran down his face.
His heart was filled with sorrow.
Not sure if he would live
to see a new tomorrow.

He had lost his wife,
whom he'd loved for many years.
Now he would have no one
to share with all his tears.

So I went over there
and sat upon his knee,
his arm around my shoulder
he closely held to me.

When he could bear it
he sent me on my way.
Then my mother asked me
just what I had to say.

I told her I'd said nothing,
a tear still in my eye.
I just simply sat there
and I helped him cry.

A Letter to Mom

Mother, do not weep for me
I chose this sacrifice.
To save our Nation's future
I offered up my life.

I know that you are grieving
and that your pain is great,
but please respect my wishes
as I accept my fate.

I love you very much
and pray that you will see;
the price is not too great
to preserve our liberty.

Hold your head up high.
Have pride in what I've done.
Remember that I love you.
Eternally, Your Son

Self Loathing

Darkness falls
and weighs heavy on my soul
it strangles the life
from within
and chokes out all hope

fiercely it slashes away
at the few remaining shards of happiness
until they lay
cold and lifeless
in a sea of despair

the waves of depression
wash over me now
cleansing my soul
of all hope

weakened by
the onslaught of despair
I submit to
it's awesome power
and fall
helplessly into
the dark recesses
of my own self loathing

The Cowboy

I wrangle around the living room
Roundin' up strays on this old broom.
With six guns tied around my waist
And a mess of bad guys I must chase.
I hop a long with my guns a blazin'
Never sure of what dangers I'm facin'.

An ambush is waitin' around that bend
I'll bet it's that darn Sponge Bob again.
He robbed the bank and shot Leroy
And now he'll face this mad cowboy.
I'll bring him in, now don't you fret
The day he crossed me he'll soon regret.

In Victory I ride back into town
And Ma is there waitin' as I climb down.
I recon she wants to clean up this room,
So I must surrender my faithful broom.

Questions from the Heart

I think about you often,
do you ever think of me?
Was I just a passing fancy
or were we meant to be?

The moments that we shared,
the love we thought we had.
Was it all a game to you
or are you feeling sad?

Do you ever miss me?
Did you really care?
Was I just a stitch in time
to pass while you were there?

Did you mean the words you said
or was it all a lie?
Am I truly what you want
or just another guy?

Tell me now I beg of you
release me from this pain.
Was I ever more to you
than just a silly game?

A Desperate Search

If only I could find someone
to fill this void inside,
who'd take away the emptiness
and stand here by my side.

To be my one companion
whose love would never fail.
To stop the endless drifting
of this ship without a sail.

Desperately I search,
hoping each day to find;
that one and only person
who loves me body, soul and mind.

I know she's out there somewhere.
A beacon of light for me
that guides me safely home
from this dark and dismal sea

Innocence Lost

In silence he moves
like many nights before.
To take a precious angel
and use her like a whore.

Her trust he has betrayed
to fill a void inside.
Now she has nobody
in whom she can confide.

He leaves the way he came
while silently she weeps,
unable to reveal
this secret that she keeps.

He says they won't believe her.
That she can never tell,
how he comes in nightly
and makes her life a Hell.

Her innocence is lost
and she can only cry.
But silently she wishes
that her Dad would die.

Someone

Can there be a Someone
who's out there just for me?
Searching just as I am
for love to set her free.

Is she out there dreaming
of a man she can't find?
One who'll love her deeply,
her body, soul and mind

Will I ever meet her?
I haven't any clue.
How do you find the one
who makes your heart beat true?

So the search continues
a journey with no end,
till I find my Someone,
My Lover and My Friend.

A Lovers Quandary

Does she or does she not?
I honestly don't know.
She says she does with words,
but never lets it show.

How can I really tell,
what she's feeling inside,
when all her emotions
she consistently hides.

I gaze into her eyes,
searching for a spark.
In a faint hope to prove
that I am in her heart.

Yet I can only see
a blank and loveless stare.
So why should I believe
that for me she does care?

In a lover's quandary
I continue to be,
wondering more and more,
does she really love me?

A Heart of Despair

Can this be real?
I wish that I knew.
This pain I feel,
how can it be true?

I do not bleed.
There is not a bruise.
Yet, there is pain;
hence, I'm confused.

The pain in my chest
invades my being,
Yet no outward signs
shall you be seeing.

Except, just perhaps,
the look in my eye
the very moment
I break down to cry.

A heart of despair
just longing to see
a lover's soft glance
to set his pain free.

Would You Notice

This photonegative slice
in hues of black and gray
represents a life,
that's sadly gone astray.

Walking in the darkness,
alone and full of doubts.
A heart so dark and lonely
is unable to cry out.

Poor decisions made,
their course now firmly set;
lead me down this road
of heartache and regret.

Blind am I, to their eyes.
I wonder if they'll see,
when I step off this curb
so that bus will set me free.

Drifting now, above this scene,
in flashing lights of red.
My shell I leave behind
unable to turn a head.

Take a Walk with Me

The moon shone down upon us
where the ocean met the shore.
As we lay there on the sand
and dreamt of what's in store.

Gently blew the ocean breeze
that coolly kissed your cheek.
A chill ran through your body,
so I helped you to your feet.

I put my arms around you
in a strong and warm embrace.
Then gently brushed aside the hair,
which had blown into your face.

In your eyes there was a longing
to feel your lover's touch.
I kissed your neck and whispered,
I love you, oh so much.

We walked along the shore
as waves came crashing in.
While softly glowed the moonlight
on your alabaster skin.

We paused for just a moment
to watch this peaceful scene.
Then you softly whispered,
is this really just a dream?

Awakened from my slumber
in this cold and lonely place.
I close my eyes again
so that I may see your face.

The First Taste of Passion

The night is cool and crisp
the stars are shining bright.
Passion's scent is on the air,
Could this be the night?

Her eyes they do entice me,
they call me to her side.
And so I move in closer
my love I must confide.

Sitting there beside her,
our eyes locked in embrace.
I reach out to her slowly,
and gently touch her face.

Her skin is smooth and silky.
Her lips as red as wine.
I lean into her slowly,
and press her lips to mine.

Passion's fire ignites.
And from that single kiss,
two hearts start a journey,
towards that carnal bliss.

Gently I caress her,
my hands so softly glide,
along her neck and shoulders,
Then slowly down her side.

Her body starts to tremble.
Her heart begins to race.
I open up her essence,
and have a little taste.

She begins to lose control,
Her feelings she can't hide.
She's pleading to me madly,
to bring my love inside.

And in that precious moment,
when the two are joined as one.
Our passions are ignited,
and burn hotter than the sun.

None will ever live more,
in our memories...
Than this very first one,
Shared by you and me.

Mary Ford Humphrey

I was born and raised in Jacksonville, Fla. I have been writing poetry since the early 80's. I have two children and two grandchildren. I love writing poetry and I feel that if I can touch one person's life, then I have accomplished something with my life. I would like to dedicate these books to my family and friends who have encouraged me in my writing. Thank you one and all.

A Helping Hand

He sat there so shattered,
dejected, and torn.
With his face in his hands,
his world blown apart.
His family was gone,
his home was no more.
His little heart had been ripped,
to its very core.
When he raised his head,
and I looked into his eyes;
I saw such terror,
it made my poor heart cry.
A single tear rolled down his face,
a tear that showed how his heart did ache.
I held my hand out to him,
and asked him for his name.
He placed his little hand in mine,
and said his name was Sean.
I gave him a little smile and said,
"Hello Sean, you can call me Grandpa John".

Life

We get into the same old rut,
each and every day.
We need to change a little bit,
somewhere along the way.
So get out there and do some things,
you've never done before.
You never know how short life is,
until the breath of life you have no more.

Angry Words

You get angry and speak in hast,
and hurt the one you love.
Mean, vicious, and cruel words,
that cannot be taken away.
So before you speak, stop and think,
of what you are about to say.
For one day words will be spoken to you
that cannot be taken away.

Unselfish Love

I walked along the beach today,
to see the little boy at play.
His footprints are so tiny,
so beautiful to see.
I watch the waves come up,
and wash them all away.
I am close enough to hear him,
His squeals of sheer delight.
He runs down to the waters edge,
to try to catch the waves;
and when it comes rolling back,
He runs and squeals' and tries to get away.
His hair is just as black, as a raven's wing,
His eyes are emerald green.
His little giggles and laughter,
Does make my happy heart sing.
I can tell they love him,
and show him in every way.
It breaks my heart to see him,
on this special day.
For I gave birth to that little boy,
Two years ago today.

All Alone

This heavy burden on my heart
has been here from the very start.
I feel so empty deep inside,
since the day your love for me just died.
You've taken away my hopes and dreams,
with all your devious lies, your schemes.
I feel so helpless and alone,
to be thrust out on my very own.
No one knows the pain, the fear;
only those who've experienced all the lonely tears.
With God's great hand, one day will come,
when I will rise above what you have done.
Of all the pain since you have gone,
the worst by far is being alone.

Garden of Love

We walk along the pathway,
and the flowers start to unfold.
Their beauty does surround us,
my hand you do enfold.
I feel your love around me,
from the look deep in your eyes.
I see them sparkle with laughter,
in hope and promise to.
For there a reflection of the love,
I give right back to you.
The years, they will not change it.
The miles, not take it away,
for it will grow ever stronger,
with each passing day.
Just like this garden around us,
that will forever grow;
our love will last forever,
as its pedals do unfold.

The People

They were here so long ago,
The People of this land.
I feel their spirits all around,
in the plants, the rocks, the sand.
I feel the sacred drumbeats,
to my very soul.
It was a song of hope and love,
so very long ago.
It whispers in the valley's deep,
and in the mountains high.
It blows along the seashore,
and way up in the sky.
The years, they have not changed it,
for it whispers still today.
It is a song of hope and love,
from long ago passed days.

The Eagle's Pride

They say these colors do not run,
of this I know is true.
For we will fight unto death,
for our glorious, Red, White, and Blue.
I remember seeing the towers fall
on that fateful day,
you thought you had us whipped,
our backs up to the wall.
But out of all the dust and smoke,
the Eagle will appear.
His head held high, His wings spread wide,
and His talons ready to strike.
You think that you can take us,
by striking a little here and there;
but do not push us too hard,
or we will send you straight to Hell.

A Rainbow Color Bridge

I look upon the mountains, so way up in the sky.
I see their golden beauty, so big, so bold, so high.
The bold bright colors that touch them,
the reds, the purples, the gold.
They fuse into a rainbow of color all their own.
The colors are brighter in the morning light,
brighter than the rising sun.
It seems to say, " Wake up my child,
the day has just begun."
But in the evening, when the sun goes down,
along the mountain ridge;
the colors seem much softer,
in the rainbow color bridge.

The Cadence of Freedom

When the wind picks up the flag unfurls,
and dances in the wind.

With every movement beats the sound,
of the rope against the pole.

It's beating out the sound of freedom,
with every little tap.

The cadence that it calls
sends music to my Soul.

The tap, tap, tap of freedom rings,
from every American flagpole

The Magic of Lights

The skies are lit with a fiery green,
a shimmering, moving light.

It glides across the midnight sky,
as wispy as a fairies wing.

You can hear the hum of music,
as its heavenly chorus sings.

The beauty of it's magic,
will take your breath away,
and fill you with an inner peace,
that keeps your worries at bay.

They call it "Aurora Borealis",
the beautiful, Great Northern Lights.

So if you get to go there,
on some cold dark winter's night,
look up into the beauty,
of the lights of peace and life.

God's Guiding Light

The rain is falling from the sky,
like the tears fall from my eyes.

As time goes by and the pain gets dimmer,
my life will brighten for I can see a shimmer.

A gleam, a stream, a beam of light
that God will shine in the dark of night.

No matter what may come my way,
God's guiding light show the way.

For He is my light, my ray of hope,
and He will shine, so I must not mope.

I will be strong in my darkest night,
for He is there with His Guiding Light.

Our Love

I look into your eyes and see,
a light that shines for only me.

Your gentle touch, your warm embrace,
a tender kiss, and my heart begins to race.

The fun we have, the times we share,
lets me know how much you care.

I think about you day and night,
I want to feel you hold me tight.

For in your arms I feel safe and secure,
of this my love, I am very sure.

So look into my eyes and see,
my love for all eternity.

The Storm

The silence before the storm is here,
that eerie feel is very near.
People hurry too and fro
some try to prepare,
others just go.

The winds pickup and start to blow,
how bad it will be, no one knows.
Everyone huddles in shelters to hide,
from the howling, treacherous winds outside.
The breaking of glass, the ripping of wood,
the sounds you hear are deafening to your ears.

Then all at once the silence is here;
it brings an eerie feeling to the air.
It won't take long for the winds to return,
so while in the eye, take caution to the wind.
The wind has returned, stronger than before,
it shakes the buildings and knocks them down.
Some of them will never be found.
When the storm subsides and the calm has returned,
everyone comes out to more terror than before.

For everything is gone, it has been destroyed;
the children don't even have any toys.
But do not worry; we will do what we can,
for one day we too, may need your helping hand.

Jewell Jeffery

If anyone was named a more appropriate name like "jewell" few have more so than Jewell. Indeed this prolific and profound writer/poet is a true jewell. Being blessed with nearly as many creative gifts as a jeweled gem has facets. All shining enchantingly and captivatingly.

One is hard pressed to determine which of her creative talents are more astounding than another. Within her deeply intuitive nature, she weaves words and visions that breathe life into the intangible, magical and mystical. With such encompassing ardor they become subtly discernable and euphoric. Leaving one with the sensation of being momentarily transported to another realm; lingering on in a subtle afterglow.

Jewell's spiritual gifts are extraordinarily complex, yet undeniably invigorating, inspiring, healing and spiritually enlightening.. Some so enveloping, giving one the sense of her recording spiritual insights after an invisible commute and audience with the Divine. So entrancingly and compelling in their tone, devotion and affectation.

When it comes to her more worldly and romantic poetics, Jewell is no less adept and accomplished. Her romantic themes and imaginings, are in a class all their own. With invitations, suggestions, and anticipations expressed with emotions, feelings, desires, and passions that push the ecstasy barometer to full tilt and beyond; she has few equals. Each phrase crafted so engrossingly, they are sheer masterpieces and memories of electrifying artistry.

As if these talents were not plentiful enough for a mere mortal, Jewell is also an exceptional photographer, painter and crafts artisan. Sings in a blissful tone that is utterly beguiling and heart stirring.

Imagine all this in gem who stands all of 5'4 with eyes of blue, gregarious personality hailing from Irish/Welsh ancestry; one readily agrees this jewell shines ever beautiful and bright.

She has several books currently in the production stage, so be sure to look for them soon.

New Waters

My boat of disillusion
sits beached on dreamer's shore
while waves of disappointment
come crashing in for more

Pondering decisions
to trust in shores I've sought
again in contemplation
to question life's cruel plot

I roam a lover's boardwalk
and watch the waves crash strong
the tides of life remind of loss
play nature's saddest song

A setting sun reflecting hues
to promise golden paths
helps me recall that love resides
where newness replaced wrath

It's time to board a different boat
to sail a wondrous sea
where waves of love and life prevail
for making memories

I'll cast a net in waters new
to catch a dream or two
once upon a time I dreamt
of passion which was true

The Gift of Knowledge

In quiet depths of wonder
Beneath human facades
Beyond questioning reason
Lies an honest answer

Bequeathed endlessly
Sought by all creatures
Known by all entities
Heard by those whose spirits listen

Beyond the crimson flow
The beating of life's rhythm
Is a mighty source of light
Without the doubt of humanity

Selfish pursuit removed
Vain glory stomped out
Empty needs vanished
She gently taps the bells of life

You'll hear the tinkling rings
In the quiet hours of wait
Stillness is never silent
Only when you ignore her song

Judge Not

Do you care or disagree
when a heart is torn in two
do you judge and criticize
Or do you seek what's true

When other's fail to measure up
to your perfected ways
Do you correct them with your style
and go on with your day

Puffed up pride and arrogance
will only push away
this person that you deem so wrong
their broken heart will stay

Does it behoove the broken
to crush their wounded soul
when you kick them while their hurting
they never will be whole

Envisions of their failure
evade your shallow mind
instead of encouraging
you lash out thoughts unkind

Your proud self righteous army
kicks the wounded down
then walks away in judgment
wearing hate's ugly frown

My mind is now pondering
the hope that you'd expect
if you were to be found in their shoes
look back in retrospect

The way you've sought to condemn
when others fail you know
do you expect the planted seeds
will reap you what you sow

Spirit

Your spirit of love:
as a slow carousel ride,
a stroll along the beach
or a gentle wind upon my face
in an early morning awakening,
soft flowing trickling streams
or the music of the breeze
rustling through trees,
a mighty fortress
and surreal refuge

Your spirit of fortitude:
as a gushing waterfall
gusts of earth shattering wind,
crashing waves upon my being
bursting treacherous flames
an instant collision
a determined force

Your spirit of life:
as the first budding of a spring rose,
the gentle breath of a newborn,
a wild flower meadow;
the view from a riverside,
fresh fallen snow
capping mountain peaks,

Your kindred spirit:
a mirrored image of heart and soul:
a knowing,
sense of belonging,
Peace deeper than understanding,
unity beyond oneness
the beauty of being
whole

A Dream, Altered

I asked for a miracle
in naive anticipation
and waited,
expecting little,
thinking it a mere wish
which dreamers such as I
long for repeatedly.

Untouched
by life's painful realities
in my everyday experiences,
I believed
that with enough faith,
I would one day hold it
in my hands
or in my heart.

Then quietly,
without fanfare,
a new day dawned before me,
awakened by promise,
and more than a mere dream
that would one day be fulfilled.

I became aware of such
passion, a longing
for knowledge,
an understanding within
without which
I realized, I would die.

Since that moment
of awakening,
newness abounds.
I see it in all that exists and lives;
becoming part of me
with each breath I take.

I inhale exhilaration,
I exhale love.
The miracle I believed in
is the miracle of love
I will cherish forever.

That day I
came to know-
miracles do exist.

Resplendent Grace

A universe, magnificent,
A suspended glowing moon,
illuminant in every evening sky,
A wonder filled galaxy
reflects over crystalline waters
musical streams trickle into roaring rivers,
waterfalls cascading over sturdy rocks,
splendorous majestic mountains
taking their stance;

The Master of creation knows
each minute grain of sand,
nestled blades of grass,
He even numbered the hairs on our heads.
He knows when the sparrow sings;
creating a backup chorus for the morning dove
and allows the crickets to assume
Dusk's gentle lullaby.

The orchestration of every heart beat,
each life giving drop of crimson,
flowing through our tiny veins,
each steady breath, whether labored or free,
our thoughts in the waking hours
and those when we lie down at night.
Why, then, do we worry
when all around us is seemingly
out of our finite control?

May we relinquish fear into the able hands
of a loving God of sacrifice.
We must abandon what attempts to bind us,
surrender to Him, who, above all,
is capable to do far more
than we can even think or imagine.

Rose Among Thorns

The faded rose may haunt it seems
reminding you of broken dreams.
Take this vision in your mind
and let it be there to remind,
To take you to a better place
where mercy sits and grace awaits.

A wisdom will come forth to you,
Flourish now in hope and truth
The petals fell among the thorns
a soft cushion for burdens worn,
They'll cover pain with silky touch,
shield your eyes that cry so much.

The petals bleed in crushed regret
and cover sin and sorrow met
They represent the blood that fell
You will not see eternal hell.
Let the petals of this rose
remind you of a love that grows

Within your heart and in your soul,
only love can make you whole.
Nurture now the love within,
It grows from pain, rebuking sin,
Revealing truth among the thorns,
your weary heart will not stay worn.

Picture now the thorns that lie
in a heap where demons cry
Where once upon a crown of thorns
in irony new life was born
Cultivate this love divine
Your petals wait in bright sunshine
open up to love anew
Let God's spirit shine through you.

Music for the Eyes

How could I help a deaf man hear
In his silence draw him near
I'd pound a song upon a drum
So he could sense where rhythm's from

His eyes would now become his ears
I'd sing him music of the spheres
With my movements he would sway
Until I took his fears away

I'd sign to him a special verse
With my body I'd converse
My moves would be symbolic dance
Remove him from his idle trance

My fingers tapping on his skin
Awake anew a sound within
When in his silence he comes near
I'll know I taught his eyes to hear

More Than Sight

How could I help the blind man see
If he sat in the same room with me
I'd paint a picture with my words
And touch his soul with what he heard

I'd speak to him in metaphors
to make his darkened spirit soar
I'd sing a song of pleasantries
until he's bowing at the knees

To make his ears become his eyes
I'd sing to him a lullaby
I'd softly whisper of romance
and watch his heart begin to dance

With his hands I'd let him see
my tender femininity
Allowing him to gently touch
the beauty he desires so much

The fragrance of a sweet perfume
would tell him I was in the room
As his words turned into sighs
I'd know his ears became his

Colorful Dance

Desert daybreaks
A misty morning
The first frostings linger
Autumn silently speaks
In frozen teardrops
Lying upon a window pane

Her season's song
Has just begun
The first stanza interrupted
By nature's cool message
Winter's rudeness prevailed
Only for a moment

Newly yellowed leaves
Glisten in golden hues
Enhancing the sunrise glow
Crystal shimmering outlines
Morning's imprint

A dance has begun
Two seasons join hands
The morning song breezes in
Harmonious melody
Nature's angelic hosts
Sing along

Listen

My serenity beckons yours
To be still together
In the quiet of our day

When silence bids us
To listen to life's rhythm
Until it becomes
As the pounding of a drum

We shall dance a tango
With our words
Your thoughts I welcome
As I hold back the cascade
Of treasures that lie within me

For it is time
to enjoy you
Enlighten me
with all that is you

Those endearments
You hold
preciously quiet

I am listening

Your serene call
Rings like a blessed melody
Upon my spirit

Victory in Defeat

Broken promises
sit atop the pieces
of my shattered heart
shouting a victor's song

You sing off key
this annoying composition
as I cover my
offended ears
with my gentle hands

Your ignorance is evident
when you don't see that victory sits
at the bottom of the rubble
in the anticipation
of my colorful spirit

The pieces of my
shattered heart
reflect a tiny ray of sun
which glistens a sparkle
of promising light

I am gathering
the shattered pieces
and creating fine art
out from the rubble
I rise again, improved

For this I shall
bestow thanks to you
The colors that
you stained my heart with
became the tool
for completion

Who Wins

Uncertainty
now leaves me baffled;
Befuddlement
my middle name.
Bewildered at
conclusions jumped to,

I muddle through
this maze called love,
Mystified by
lack of action.
Perplexity
chokes out
my expectations,

Numb with dismay
The only certainty
Is my foolish persistence
at convincing one of
my genuineness.

My heart in disarray
by the havoc caused
by disbelief
in pure intentions.

My wasted songs
have become a medley
of sad show tunes
It is now time
to tell the band
they played out of time.

The Romantic Play
has been canceled
until further notice
Rain checks available
at naïveté.com

The Bride's Song

Entwine souls with me
The dance of desire
Awaits life's joy
Lay naked and unashamed
Along side my freedom

Be my beam
of radiating light,
an alchemy like no other.

You are my chalice
filled with invigoration
Such sweet wine of life
Somehow seems decadent
But it is ours freely

You are the delicious taste
For which I long
In the morning
To touch all my waiting lips

When love's countenance
Shines on a new day
You brighten life
With an aura
that is only you

Alone
I am whole
I am oneness
in spirit

Yet our togetherness
compliments
What is already true

Masculine Beseeches Feminine

Your glorious beauty
Blossoms daily renewal
Each daydream glides
Into nightfall's embrace
Nature's own nuance
Are factors of awareness

Seeds of blessings planted
Watered by your caring tears
Trickle over my heart's garden path
Like a stream in the desert -
Such elegance
~ my oasis~

Your delicate petals beckon In sweet fragrance
Eloquence bequeaths each breath
Your verses become an elixir
sent to the atmosphere
to be cherished by the angels

Sing to me fair maiden
Love goddess of the night
So I may just once
Soak in your heart's melody
In hopes of capturing the bliss
Of your soul's erotic splendor

Feminine Beseeching Masculine

Illustrious blazing splendor
elegant grace beyond the norm
Unique by today's shallow standard
is feminine eminence

May I charm your masculine mind
And take your thoughts
on a journey less traveled
where beauty lines each path

With graceful movement
fashioned by unique confidence
without haughtiness or ego
Luxurious eloquence beseeches you

Compassionate yearning
desires to surround your muscular being
Rest in this—my heart's desire
My passion will not deny your need

May we lie in our created ecstasy
Quivering utopia in the glow
of a silvery moonbeam
As our spirits become one

Love Drought

This need within is deep
I am consumed by an empty void
My longing is as a hollow river bed
waiting for someone to come
do a rain dance at my feet

Then why do I fear the flood
when early trickles of love begin
with a slow methodical rhythm
tapping on my soul's window pane?

My heart has cried out for too long
to be refreshed with love's libation
I can smell the fragrance
begin to fill the air
as my heart's door is opened
yet the storm door of protection
keeps it from getting my feet wet

When fear comes in
like a threatening flood
on my dry, parched heart
I ache for the refreshing rain of certainty
of a forever downpour of love

I will toss this fear into the air
until it dissipates into the past
I do recognize the dam that sits
in the way of passion's floodgate

I hold the key in my tender hand
and begin to unlock the gate
I see you on the other side
Perhaps I shall start the rain dance myself
I extend this invitation to you
with a gentle tapping on your heart's door...

Shall we dance?

Unsatisfied

Voracious
Left in longing
This void screams from
a hollow cave which is my soul
Echoing my cries of the night
Despair takes its stance
in the pit of my being
Dissatisfied with selfish gain
My spirit unsettled

Lover of my soul
Surround me
Saturate where I am dry
There is no hunger
You cannot satisfy
One tiny morsel to my lips
is like finest chocolate
Each promising word
a golden nugget

Please receive my tears
Place them in the River of Life
Give them a purpose
for the washing of the wounded
Turn them to waterfalls of beauty

Let them be a fountain of refreshment
for those who thirst for more
Place each drop
Carefully one at a time
to the tip of parched tongues
Allow me to see
they are not in vain

Serenity Beckons

Silence
bids me to listen.
The stillness
begs me to sing,
the song asks
for my hand in a dance;
sometimes I dance
Alone.

When alone,
silence re-enters,
becoming my comforter.
My spirit sings,
my heart dances,
I am
Whole.

In stillness,
I trust.
Abundant peace,
tranquil thoughts,
a knowing
that life can be,
all that is
Serenity

A Woman of Worth

For her,
every day is a gift.
Blessings are expected.
Her faith sustains.

She contains wisdom
derived from experience.
Her strength,
gained from trials.

An authentic personality
attracts others to her presence.
Empty words never pass her lips.
Her pursuits, not in vain,

Assumption is
neither practiced or tolerated.
She understands that
jealousy and greed destroy
herself and others,

Challenges are embraced,
Dignity, her character,
Integrity, a way of life,
Her intentions, pure

Her counsel is sure.
Her goals, for betterment,
She celebrates her difference
and knows the fine line
between pride and prideful.

Well aware that forgiveness
is the balm that heals,
patience is a virtue,
and the shadows of night
never feel her wrath.

Lead the Way

Guide me through
this darkened world
spiritual visions to explore,
Awaken my senses to
enchanting possibilities.
May I invite exhilaration
and edification
without apprehension,

Aid me
to ignore the detestable
which attempts to surround
our existence.
Let me examine
what is disheartening
in order to gain
wisdom with purpose,
to enlighten hardened hearts.

May my ways be gratifying
to wounded souls,
my words enriching
to empty ears.

I will listen wholeheartedly
for new songs in the morning,
I will sing from my spirit
what is held in my heart,
with all my might,
for the purpose of
others singing along.

David Frey Josephson

David Frey Josephson was born and bred in Australia growing up in sunny Brisbane. He graduated from University with a bachelor of Business and pursued a management career. His job requires an analytical and logical approach with decisions based on reason. Recently, he has found his creative side, which has opened the door to his spirituality. A find for which he is most grateful.

The Worrier

He stands before me, the worrier
His weapons sharp and fine

He stands before me, the worrier
What's his is now mine

He shows strength and courage
He's stoic and proud

He guards and protects
No weakness allowed

His mood is constant
His shield is his heart

His gestures are frequent
His stance set apart

He competes with a vengeance
Till the victories are won

His efforts are tireless
Till revelry is done

Stand before me, my worrier
Lay your head upon my chest

Stand before me, my worrier
It's Time to take rest

The Song of Squeals

My mates and I, we ate some food
They pushed us in a truck
The mum's and dad's they stayed behind
And wished us all good luck

We jostled, joked and mucked about
With excitement in the air
The trip was long, the air was hot
But little did we care

We slept the night in the strangest place
Where lots of trucks had come
The place was clean, no mud, no slop
And room for everyone

Morning came and something's wrong
The air is full of fear
Panic starts to grip us now
We don't know why we're here

We hear the calls from out in front
And the closer they become
We think of home and all we know
And realize we are done

We look around and see our eyes
And wonder what's for real
And as we move in one by one
We sing our song of squeals

The Art of Thought

Upon reflection of visions
is the thinking of art
through insight of images
And the minds of creation

upon visions of reflection
Is the art of thinking
through images of insight
and the creation of minds

The Gift

In the quiet of his thoughts
The innocence of his dreams
Alone in rhythmic calm
And nothing's what it seems

Noise abruptly wakes him
His body sleeps away
His mind plays a game
The memories here to stay

Clouds rush past a restless time
And blocks a hopeful light
Wind blows his calm away
He vanishes out of sight

She calls him from a distance
Her voice caresses his face
He hears her whispered offer
She gives with all her grace

Her spirit quietly wake him
His body sweeps away
His mind plays a jingle
A melody's here to stay

Clouds dance past a restful time
And opens a hopeful light
Wind blows the dark away
He emerges into sight

She calls him from a closeness
Her lips caress his face
He accepts her whispered offer
Together they share a grace

And in the quiet of his thoughts
Awakening of his dreams
A union in rhythmic calm
And everything's what it seems

The Forward Movement

He shuffles slowly through the dust
His legless body leaving a snail trail
His arms strong from dependence
His hands worn like feet
Flies find his open moistness
Fluttering wings blur his sight
His swollen tongue fills his mouth
Dusty dryness coats his throat
Morning sun heats his nakedness
And cracks his unwashed skin
Sores of pus rack his body
And infection waits its turn
He excites to see his rusty friend
A playful time of sorts
The mortar shell, a makeshift toy
A companion, bitter sweet
Momma lifts and holds him
Trickles water on his lips
He smiles from the comfort
His day has just begun

....

The products of us
Are the mongers of war
Hostilities, aggression
We opened the door
Generations of progress
Betterment of kinds

Mentors for guidance
The questioning of minds
The evolution of spirit
Each donation a gift
A cumulative growth
For an ancestral shift
The seeds can be sewn
The peace lines drawn
The modern day Gandhi's
Are yet to be born

The Birth of Logic

He scrounges for food
And scurries to his cave
His body is tired
His heart is so brave
He rubs his rough skin
Mud mixed with course hair
The cold rushes in
And chills the night air
He grunts with discomfort
His anger a roar
He runs in a frenzy
His mind is at war
He bangs down a rock
Hot sparks flick away
Watching with interest
His black turns to grey
His head turns aside
A musing of sorts
He ponders his question
His emergence of thought

Near

In the corners of his eyes
The daily traffic dances
Caution holds his vision
Dreaming takes it's chances
In the calm of no reason
Of logic or clear thought
A conflict of some places
Where wishes hold the court
Amongst the throngs of every kind
The living angels smile
The message on their faces
Is be here just a while
Within the light above their heads
The golden ambers glow
The colors share a feeling
A direction where to go
In the corners of his mind
A memory plays a tune
The lyrics seem familiar
The calling will be soon

Glorious Food

I DREAM OF A SCALLOP
A LIFE FROM THE SEA
SO DELICATE AND TENDER
TO SATISFY ME
THE JUICIEST OF CORN
SITTING PLUMP ON THE COB
EATING'S A TASK
BUT WELL WORTH THE JOB
THE MAJESTY OF PUMPKIN
HAVE IT MANY WAYS MADE
PREFER IT TO BE ROASTED
BUT CAN EASILY BE SWAYED
THE MAGNITUDE OF THE PEA
COMPLIMENTS ANY DISH
EATEN IN NUMBERS
IF ONLY I WISH
SAY YES TO SALMON
IT'S NICE TO SHARE
EAT WITH MY FRIEND
DREAMERS WILL DARE
LIFE WITHOUT MANGO
LIFE WITHOUT TASTE
SAVIOUR THE FLAVOUR
EAT WITHOUT HASTE
THE SWEET OF CHOCOLATE

THE TASTE IS SO DREAMY
A TREAT FOR ALL AGES
SO SMOOTH AND SO CREAMY
THE CRUNCH OF APPLE
A FRIEND FROM THE PAST
I MENTION IT NOW
ALTHOUGH IT IS LAST
AFTER ALL THIS TALKING
MY TONGUE'S IN MY CHEEK
MY TUMMY IS RUMBLING
THINK I'LL EAT FOR A WEEK

The Meeting

Walking through a bustling crowd
A journey to a friend
It's purpose has no logic
But the story had no end

Looking through busy faces
A blur of all unmet
Searching for the familiar
A face you can't forget

The world around just stops
As our wandering eyes once meet
A warmness rush engulfs us
From our hands down to our feet

We know that look we give
We've seen it once before
A look we can remember
Which is why we wanted more

A nervous touch that follows
An embrace that won't let go
A bodies' shaking happening
A love, that is on show

What was before has meaning
Our present is romance
Our future is uncertain
Until we take a chance

Tom Zart

It's appropriate and symbolic that the romantic poet Tom Zart was born on Valentines Day in Topeka, Kansas in 1945. His youth confronted adulthood many times by working on the family farm or helping his parents in their business. In the early fifties family roots were planted in the famous Plaza section of Kansas City which was walking distance to nearby Westport. He lived there for six months of the year then went to work on their 140-acre Bonner Springs farm the other six months. It was a learning experience that proved invaluable to The Westport Poet.

Westport is a historic section of Kansas City, Missouri renown for its modern nightlife and shops and its noble past as a trading post, a transportation hub and a civil war battle. It was in Westport, amid the war memorial plaques, the fountains and nature that Tom wrote his first poem, Thunder In The Ground, a civil war ode to the men who died in the war. His inspiration came from an inscription on a civil war memorial.

Zart's poetic endeavors soon began to proliferate along with his subject matter. Tom, an addicted romantic, and history buff, began writing poems about love, religion and patriotism. His early inspirations came while working at the railroad for 30 years. Zart would utilize his time on those long railroad trips gleaning all that he could from his senses: the haunting sound of the train, its whistle and the long hours gazing out at the sunset and the pastoral settings fleeting by, of farmhouses and cities whose inhabitants he would never know.

He took notes of his coworker's experiences, especially the veterans who told their stories of the horror of war and their sacrifice in World War II, Korea, and especially, Viet Nam.

The Westport Poet lived vicariously in their spirit and told their stories in his poems. Tom Zart, who has a distinctive God given vocal talent, would recite his stories and poems at various social events and bistros around the Westport area. His audience was always enthralled and he soon was in demand and they named him-The Westport Poet.

His abilities have not gone without notice. He has been published by numerous magazines and his poems were featured weekly in over 215 newspapers across our country with an estimated readership of 6 ½ million for approximately 5 years. Tom has performed his poems live on radio shows from New York to California.

All Poets Serve a Master

Most poets have a bit of Solomon
Shakespeare and Poe within.
Constantly eager to share their visions
of love, life, joy and sin.

Some guzzle whiskey
some sip wine,
some prefer cola
and feel just fine.

Some smoke pot
or suck cigarettes,
some abuse drugs
with lifetime regrets.

Some attend church
and sing of God,
while others make fun
and call them odd.

All have a purpose,
which drives them to compose.
All serve a master,
who by free will, they chose.

Little Baby

Little baby, I love you
for you are a part of me.
Each and every inch you'll grow
I want to be there to see.

Someday you'll chase fireflies
who ride the breath of the winds.
Someday you'll be all grown up
and out on the town with friends.

You have your daddy's freckles;
you've got your mommy's eyes.
I pray to God every day
you'll survive all of life's lies.

Little babies shoot up fast
as they need to stretch and grow.
They do such things as children do
in a world they've yet to know

Someday you will understand
how your parents feel inside.
Someday you'll have your babies
and raise them with great pride.

Of all the gifts that life may bring,
a sweet baby is still the best.
Your mom and I shall love you
'Till the day we're laid to rest.

The Loneliness of War

I know I'm still here so far, far away,
as I fight for what I believe is right.
I wonder about you and your mom,
every moment of every day and night.

The loneliness of war can drive you insane,
if you don't get letters of concern from home.
Left, right, behind and ahead,
Death awaits leaving love ones alone.

We pray to God that we will be saved
to return home or live the here after.
Bloody, dirt-covered men, we see everyday,
as we yearn for those times of laughter.

The far off stare of a fallen comrade,
as you stay by his side till his end.
No mother ever carried her infant child,
more carefully than we do a friend.

Many have their own personal diaries,
to help keep their faculties together.
Watching hot steel crash into human flesh,
Always make home seem far away and better.

I've become an expert at dodging, weaving and diving,
so try not to worry too much about me.
Just help your mom and stand up from the ground,and while I'm
gone be all you can be.

Love Dad

A Good Poem

A good poem paints a picture
for both your heart and brain.
It doesn't need a second chance
to make its meaning plain.

A good poem is like the flower,
the lily or the rose.
God plants it in a poet's brain
and there its beauty grows.

A good poem like a cardinal
is pregnant with song;
you can't help but hear its message
as it sings what's right or wrong.

A good poem helps us remember
what the joys of life are for;
it makes us want to love someone
'Till death comes knocking at our door

Forever More

I love to be loved in the morning
I love to be loved at night.
I love to be loved anytime
for love in the darkness is light.

I pray every day to say thank you
for all I have others do not.
I pray every day cause I'm guilty
for I don't deserve what I've got.

Your love is the best of the rest
for your mission in life is me.
Once I was selfish and cruel
but fearing your loss made me see.

God gave Eve to Adam
To smile and suffer no more.
God gave you to me
I will love you forever more.

Our Mother's Love

Our mother's love, like a candle,
Burns brightly upon the shelf.
As she lights the way for all others,
never thinking of herself.

Seven little kids in a farmhouse
by my moms' hard work survived.
Through her love and faith in Jesus,
We learned how to struggle and strive.

The lilacs still bloom by the window
where our mom would quilt and sew.
In the winter she'd sing by the fire
to the tunes she thought we should know.

Our father labored at a quarry
in the dust of the earth every day.
He worked so hard for his money
for the bills our family must pay.

Little sister came down with pneumonia
and almost died in bed.
Our momma lie sick beside her
Putting cool rags on her head.

We were sure glad to see daddy's face
as he drove up our driveway.
He ran up and into the house,
then knelt by their bed to pray.

"Oh, Lord, please save my family
from the fever that burns within
for we have always loved Jesus
and will serve him till our end"

Our mother and sister survived,
But, daddy, he died long ago.
When it's our time for heaven,
we'll see many that we know.

God's Poets

The prize jewels of any nation
are the philosophers of the heart.
How they think is universal,
for it's God who makes them so smart.

Most poets tell the truth of life,
though they may wrap it in beauty.
It's their passion, not their purpose;
to compose is but their duty.

Poets have no reason to lie
when the truth is always so clear.
All that others say and do
is but food for the poet's ear.

One merit of a poet's work,
which most people cannot deny,
they say more and in fewer words
to illuminate you and I.

God sent his poets down to earth
with words of wisdom and of worth,
that they might touch the souls of sin
and bring them back to Him again.

God has always had his poets,
who he watches with love from space.
But Satan has his poets too,
who try to lead us from our grace.

King Solomon was a poet,
who spoke of love, life, death, and war.
That lips were like threads of scarlet,
and that breasts were roses and more.

The wild birds sing and flowers bloom,
as clouds form figures in the sky.
But only humans will write poems,
that shall last long after they die.

The eldest sister of all arts,
which some have called the devils wine.
Poetry is but pure passion,
to stimulate the heart and mind.

Pathways

Lord, I'm so lonely, I thirst everyday
In search of the love I need,
like a man in prison with no warmth at night,
A slave who seeks to be freed.

For I need a woman who will heal my heart,
so my life won 't seem so wrong.
I'll lie down beside her and gamble again,
then sing of our love in a song.

Remember, young Adam, your first favorite born,
who slept in your garden alone.
You took form his body and transformed some flesh,
then gave him a woman unknown.

Whichever the pathway I should choose to take,
I realize that there will be brambles.
For the man who has visions everyday of his life,
Will always be the same who gambles.

Now, to heaven I pray, for my treasure of life,
after searching the deserts in vain.
I'm tired of mirages from fool-hearted women,
Please give me someone who's sane.

May her eyes be turquoise with cheeks like peaches,
Ripe and ready to risk?
Soon they'll turn rosy when she sneaks a peek
to the tingle of where I kiss.

Though I will love her, I shall never follow.
Nor will I ever lead.
I'll walk beside her and share all I have
for the children who spring from seed.

If we should argue about foolish things,
I 'd rather be loved than right.
Then when I lie down at the end of my day,
I'll sleep with a smile at night.

Shoulder to Shoulder

Americans harmonize in sentiment
while facing the challenges of life.
Shoulder to shoulder we defined our land
through hardship, sacrifice and strife.

We are eager to oppose our enemies
wherever they raise their head.
Our principles must be practiced
to avoid being conquered or dead.

We fail to see the merits of a dictator
only freedom to work and pray as we please.
Most seek guidance from a higher power
as we share our concerns on our knees.

We can't foresee what the future may bring
though we give it our best not to fail.
Every 4th of July we illuminate the sky
Proving freedom is alive and well.

Divine Intervention

I never write a poem
that doesn't write itself.
I catch a buzz and come alive
like a puppet off it's shelf.

Hearing many voices,
whose words are never mine.
My pen becomes a painter's brush
Forming visions on a line.

I seem to be a better person,
when it's time to sit down and write.
A higher power guides my hand,
Sharing wisdom by day and night.

People born to create,
Have no choice but to perform.
It's the rush of sharing their gift,
that elevates them from the norm.

What would our world become,
without intervention from above?
Angry beings in a revolving cage,
with no sense of passion or love.

Wings of Heaven

It's a wonderful situation
to be in love with you.
All my thoughts have changed
Because of everything you do.

I lack the desire for others
No yearning for their love or favor.
All I wish is a life with you
till it's time to greet our savior.

I was afraid I would never find love
Leaving no stone unturned.
I had to suffer through stupidity
to grow from all I learned.

Life is too short to remain a fool
who doesn't see blessings handed down.
From now to judgment I will love you
till the wings of heaven whisper their sound.

The Greatest Lesson One Can Learn

The greatest lesson one can learn
is how when loved, to love in return.

Joined together through night and day
Equally yoked in work and play.

Remaining true both body and soul
Never loosing our common goal.

Sharing each other the best we can
before we are but bits of sand.

Mutual love is beyond compare
serving one another in the life we share.

Without compassion humans loose
simply by the path they choose.

Love is a miracle from God to man
how some deny it I can't understand.

The First One to Love Me

The first one to love me was you; Lord
and nothing can take that away.
My soul is refreshed by living water
while my heart flows with love each day.

I thank you for the love of my family
and I thank you for the love of my life.
I thank you for all of the blessings
you give to each husband and wife.

Your glory rides high on the sunsets;
your voice is the thunder of rain.
I thank you for all of the heavens
And Jesus who came to be slain.

I feel when your eyes are upon me
as you listen to my humble cry,
you've redeemed the soul of your servant
to dwell in your mansion on high.

I'll claim each and every promise
From the Lord of the earth and sky.
I'm so glad I'm free from my bondage
of the grave where my body shall lie.

I thank you for parting the darkness
and guiding my footsteps each day.
I thank you for being my shepherd;
you've walked with me all the way.

I know your armor protects me
from the devil in search of his feast.
And all who are lost without you
shall dwell in hell with the beast!

Soldiers

Every man should be a soldier,
as it was with Romans and Greeks,
for evil loves to steal men's souls
and strike freedom from their cheeks.

It's not the guns or armament,
or the flags which fly in parade,
But love and cooperation
that stops the devil's charade.

Always remember those who march
to the roll of muffled drums.
Many we know, shall not return
except to sleep beneath the mum

Bravery

Many brave souls lived before now,
Unwept and unknown by their face.
Lost somewhere in the distant night,
'Till a poet chronicles their grace.

True bravery is shown by performing,
without witness, what one might be
Capable of before the world,
without any or all to see.

How great the brave who rest in peace,
all blessings from heaven to earth.
They gave our country but their best,
those destined to be brave from birth.

Soldier for the Lord

I'm a solider for the Lord
who's been up and who's been down,
though while on the battlefield,
I have never turned around.

I face more than flesh and blood,
with the devil's evil hoard.
But they shall not steal my soul.
For I swing my Lord's swift sword.

I wear all of God's armor;
with helmet, breastplate and shield.
As Satan's arrows fly by
from his archers of the field.

The devil casts his dark net
over any he may charm.
He'll lead them from salvation,
with has hands upon their arm.

I battle evil daily,
and I pray that you'll join me.
We're not alone in this world,
for we're loved and watched by Thee.

Who

Who wrote the tune the songbird sings?
Who made the diamonds we wear on rings?

Who caused the snow and rain to fall?
Who made spring, winter, summer and fall?

Who gave man a woman to love?
Who made the clouds and sky above?

Who lights the stars and moon in the night?
Who makes heaven and beyond so bright?

Who gives us babies we follow till death?
Who made us able to speak with our breath?

Who gives us heroes willing to die?
Who made the tears we shed as we cry.

Who shows us hope and guides our way?
The same one who loves us night and day.

I Think of You

I think of you as I smell a rose
I think of you when I see your clothes.
I think of you if I weren't here
who would love you and call you dear.

I think of you when I'm asleep
I think of you and will me you keep?
I think of you when I kneel to pray
recalling all, which you might say.

I think of you and what you mean to me
I think of you and all you can be.
I think of you when your not home
I feel your presence whenever I'm alone.

The Murderous Hand of Man

War I hate, though not men, flags nor race,
But war itself with its ugly face.
When we lose faith in the brave which die,
then we're not fit to greet those who cry.

What distinguishes war isn't death,
But that man is slain by fellow man.
Crushed by cruelty and injustice,
with his enemy's murderous hand.

War tends to punish the punishers,
so the losers won't suffer alone.
The essence of war is but violence,
Till the survivors come marching home.

Our Flag

Our flag is fabric wove of thread,
Carried by heroes live and dead.
She stands for justice and courage too,
with her colors; red, white and blue.

For all who serve her, there'll be cheers,
for any who die, there'll be tears,
for all who love her, life is swell,
for those who harm her, war is hell.

How many moms have cried before,
as they sent their children to war.
How many dads have not returned,
because our freedom must be earned.

Wars were waged where brave men died
as patriots fought side by side.
Our flag is still the pearl of earth,
Because of those who prove her worth.

Veteran's Day

The cost of freedom is sometimes high,
Extremely more when our loved one's die.

Men and women pledged to fight and serve,
And it's our support that they deserve.

Mankind itself is the one to blame,
That all through history, the story's the same.

Peace, like love, can be hard to acquire,
Subject always to enemy fire.

Some how the righteouses tend to prevail,
over the miss-guided, prone to fail.

No wonder we fear the tongues that lie,
As mankind squabbles beneath God's sky.

The danger our solders face is real,
So lets let them know just how we feel.

Put forth your flag and show them your heart,
As those we love from us depart.